Supernatu

VAM

WEREWOLVES & DEMONS

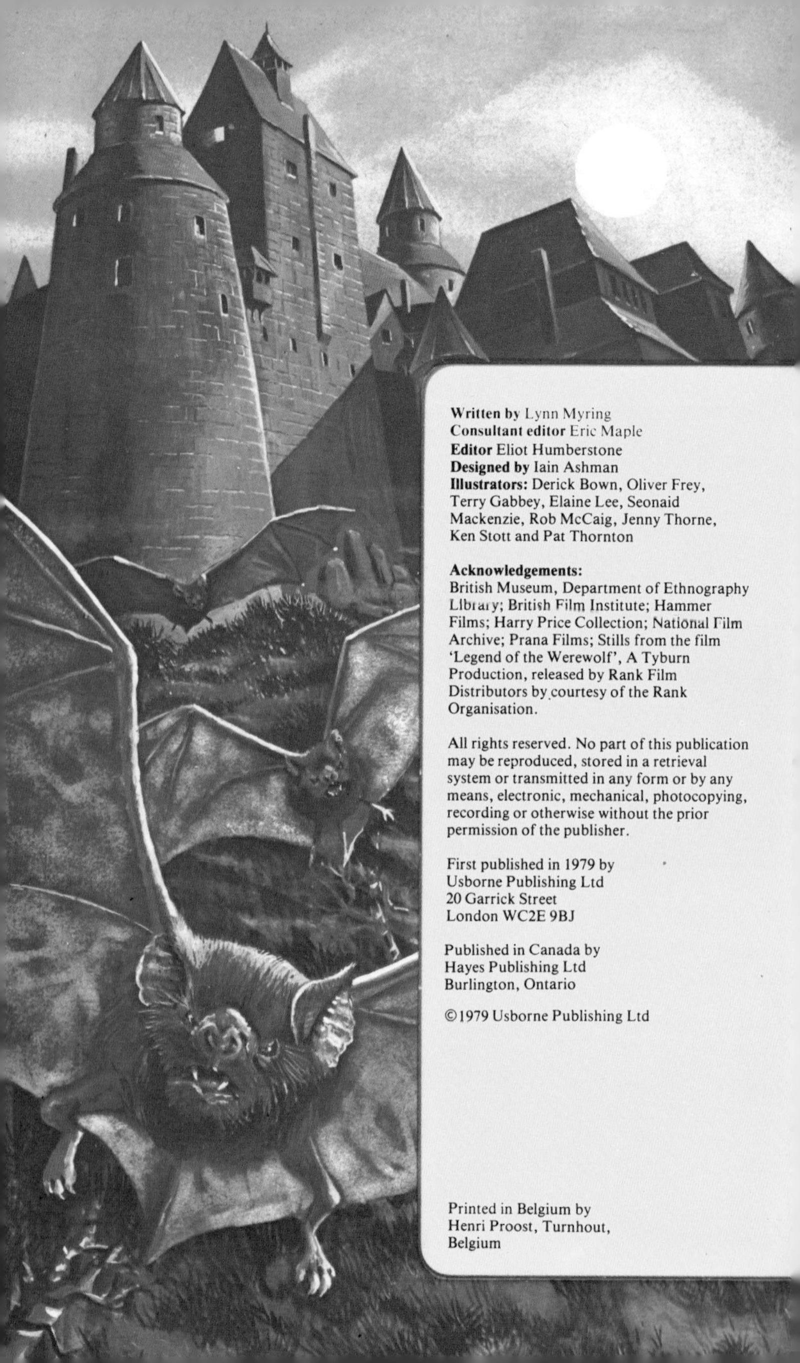

Written by Lynn Myring
Consultant editor Eric Maple
Editor Eliot Humberstone
Designed by Iain Ashman
Illustrators: Derick Bown, Oliver Frey, Terry Gabbey, Elaine Lee, Seonaid Mackenzie, Rob McCaig, Jenny Thorne, Ken Stott and Pat Thornton

Acknowledgements:
British Museum, Department of Ethnography Library; British Film Institute; Hammer Films; Harry Price Collection; National Film Archive; Prana Films; Stills from the film 'Legend of the Werewolf', A Tyburn Production, released by Rank Film Distributors by courtesy of the Rank Organisation.

First published in 1979 by
Usborne Publishing Ltd
20 Garrick Street
London WC2E 9BJ

Published in Canada by
Hayes Publishing Ltd
Burlington, Ontario

Printed in Belgium by
Henri Proost, Turnhout,
Belgium

Supernatural Guides

VAMPIRES WEREWOLVES & DEMONS

About this book

Throughout the world, stories have been told of horrible, bloodsucking creatures called vampires, and of werewolves and other werebeasts, which were people who could change into animal shapes and do evil deeds. For centuries, many people lived in fear of these evil beings. They even invented special techniques to destroy them and protect themselves.

This book contains stories based on first-hand reports by people who genuinely believed they had been attacked by vampires and werewolves. It shows how these creatures are thought to have looked and acted, and gives some of the possible reasons for these haunting and incredible legends.

Contents

What is a Vampire?

Legends of vampires and similar bloodsucking creatures come from all parts of the world. According to these legends, vampires were living corpses who returned from the dead to haunt people.

It was believed that vampires left their graves at sunset in search of victims and drank their blood. The victims were often people the vampire knew in his lifetime. Human blood was supposed to be the food that vampires needed to keep them alive.

In the past, thousands of corpses have been dug up by people searching for signs of these evil creatures.

The undead

Vampires were often thought to be violent criminals or people who had died suddenly. Anyone who committed suicide, or who was the victim of a vampire's attack, was also thought to become a vampire.

Often such a person had not had a proper burial and it was believed that the spirit, unable to go to heaven or hell, remained active in the corpse. This is why vampires were known as 'the undead'.

The most terrifying stories of vampires come from Eastern Europe—where Polish vampires, for instance, were said to float in blood-filled coffins. Their Russian relatives were supposed to take the blood from a victim's heart. Most vampires, however, preferred to attack at the neck, puncturing the skin with razor-sharp fangs until the blood flowed.

The blood preserved the vampire's body so it did not rot in the grave like an ordinary corpse. If a vampire's coffin was dug up the body looked as if it was asleep, rather than dead.

Vampires worked at night, under cover of darkness, often creeping into a bedroom while an innocent victim lay sleeping. If the victim was not completely drained of blood in an attack, the vampire would return the following evening.

The ways of the vampire

People in countries as far apart as Hungary and China have believed in the existence of bloodsucking vampires. Not all vampires behaved in the same way.

Many were thought to be able to fly or change their shape. Most were accused of attacking animals as well as humans, for blood to drink.

In some areas the vampire was a bodyless ghost. In others there were arguments about what animated the vampire corpse; an evil spirit or the return of its original soul, unable to rest in death.

▲European gypsies believed the vampire left his bones behind when he rose from the grave. He roamed around at night, waking sleepers, breaking things and making a terrible noise. He also harmed cattle by riding them at breakneck speed over the fields.

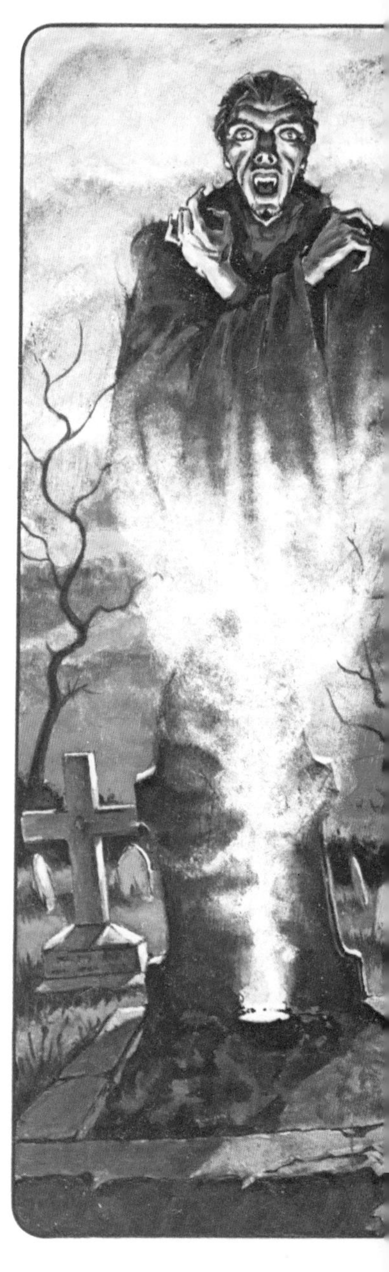

From beyond the grave

Not all vampires had to dig through the earth to reach their victims. Some were not bound by the ordinary laws of nature. They were said to escape from their graves by taking on a misty shape. In this form they could seep through the coffin and six feet of earth that covered them and become solid again above ground.

As they made no disturbance to the soil, the only sign of a vampire's resting place was the hole through which the misty body flowed. Locked doors were no problem either. Unless the wise occupant had rubbed garlic around the frame, the vampire would simply assume his misty form and slide underneath it.

▲Almost all legends tell of vampires drinking blood from the living. Some were also thought to attack fresh corpses. They not only drank the blood but sometimes even ate the flesh of a dead person. They were also blamed for spreading foul diseases.

▲Some vampires were supposed to be invisible and very spiteful, breaking anything they could get their hands on and spitting blood all over the place. These vampires beat their victims black and blue, flinging them about in an attempt to get at their blood.

Varieties of vampire

Europe was terrorized for many centuries by vampire beliefs. The Ancient Greeks feared human-like demons that drank blood from the living. The Norse people of Scandinavia believed the dead were alive in their graves, but had become evil and violent.

Vampires were not reported in Britain after 1300, but they haunted the rest of Europe for much longer. As recently as 1863 there was a vampire epidemic in Bulgaria. It did not end until a witch discovered and destroyed the evil spirit.

Monsters of the night

▲The Russian vampire (shown left), known as a 'vieszcy', gnawed his own hands and feet while in the grave but at midnight he escaped to attack cattle, seek blood and ring church bells.

The Bulgarian vampire had two forms. For the first 40 days he learned how to be evil and had a filmy body which gave off bright sparks in the dark. After this the vampire rose from the grave in his old body, but he now had only one nostril and a long sharp tongue.

◀In Transylvania, now part of central Romania, there was a vampire called the 'murony'. It could change from a human into a cat, dog, toad or any blood-sucking insect. This sort of disguise made it very easy for the murony to attack his victims, as they would not be suspicious of animals. When discovered in human form in the grave, the murony could be recognized by its long sharp nails and the fact that blood dripped from its eyes, ears, nose and mouth.

Many central Europeans believed that a soul could leave its body and enter into an animal without any ill effect, even before death. Some people thought it was dangerous to go to sleep thirsty as the soul would then go out to look for a drink. The soul often took the shape of a mouse or flying insect.

▲These three figures are types of German vampire. On the left is a 'neuntoter', blamed for spreading plague as it had such an unpleasant, smelly body and was covered in sores. In the middle is a 'dracul', a vampire corpse that was brought to life by a demon. The vampire on the right is a 'nachzehrer' which had very strange habits. It sat in its tomb holding the thumb of one hand tightly in the other, always kept its left eye open, and made loud grunting noises while it devoured its shroud.

Preventing vampires

People terrified of vampires found many ways of protecting themselves. Ointments and charms to ward off the undead were sometimes sold, but wild roses, garlic, fire and crosses were said to give the best protection.

Although it was possible to kill vampires it was far more important to try and prevent a suspect corpse becoming one and leaving its grave in the first place. A vampire's bite turned its victims into new vampires when they died. They hypnotized people while feeding on their blood so the victim remembered nothing of an attack and a vampire could return several times to drink blood, undiscovered and unfeared.

Victims of a vampire's bite were not the only corpses said to join the undead. Anyone who had a violent or mysterious death or had been very evil when alive, was thought likely to return as a bloodsucker.

Anyone at all unusual in appearance or behaviour was supposed to become a vampire. In Greece, where red hair and blue eyes are uncommon, they were said to be signs of the undead. Great care was taken with such suspects when they died and corpses were always watched and never left in the dark.

Guarding the coffin

The picture below shows a night-time scene following a death. The precautions taken against vampires illustrated here were used in many parts of Europe in the 15th and 16th centuries.

Sun and moon light were once seen as strong sources of life-giving energy, which might be able to reactivate a corpse. Curtains are still shut today if a death occurs, perhaps because of this old belief.

Being creatures of the night, the undead were terrified of lights and fires. Torches were lit outside the house and plenty of candles and a large roaring fire protected the people inside.

Vampires hated garlic and anyone who did not like it was thought rather suspicious. It was hung around rooms, rubbed onto doors, window frames and even farm animals to ward off vampires.

Animals were a great danger to the unburied corpse. If one jumped over the coffin, the body inside was sure to become one of the bloodsucking undead. Even the animal might turn into a vampire at death.

Mirrors were thought to reflect the soul and were taken down or turned to face the wall near a corpse. This was to prevent the soul becoming trapped in the mirror and returning later to animate the body.

Burying a vampire

Some burial customs still observed today may have started as ways of keeping the undead in the grave.

Flowers were first put in or on coffins in the belief that they would bind the spirit and prevent it coming back to haunt the living. Wild roses were used when dealing with vampires.

Graves were dug deep, so that plenty of earth held down the corpse if it tried to escape. Graves were also marked out, as walking over a corpse was said to turn it into a vampire.

▲People who committed suicide were thought to become vampires. They were pinned in the coffin with a stake and buried at the crossroads. This was done to confuse the vampire, so he would not find his way home to attack family and friends.

▲Heavy stones were placed over the vampire's grave to prevent it climbing out. Where piles of rocks were used in place of a single big boulder, travellers were supposed to add a stone or two if they did not want to be chased home by the vampire.

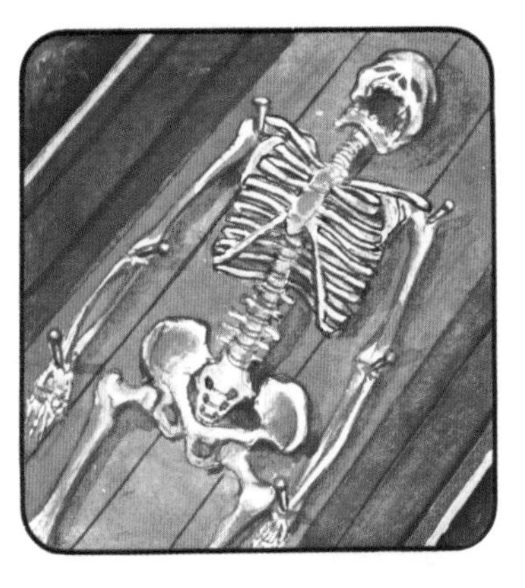

▲Skeletons have been discovered riveted to the graves like the one shown above, or with their leg-bones broken to stop the corpse walking. Sometimes red ochre was painted on in the hope that this blood-coloured clay would satisfy the need for real blood.

At the grave-side

If people suspected they were haunted by a vampire they searched the graveyard for the blood-drinking beast.

Once it was found, there were many ways of killing a vampire. These varied from place to place, but a common method was to drive a stake into its heart with a single blow. Sometimes red-hot nails replaced the stake and they were often hammered into the head as well. Ripping a vampire's heart from its body to boil in oil or beheading it with a gravedigger's spade made quite certain that it could not rise again from the grave.

The picture below shows some of the precautions taken when a vampire was found, or someone thought likely to turn into one was buried. The body was staked face down into the coffin so it could not climb out. Crosses of willow wood were put under the arms and holy water sprinkled in the grave to repel evil demons which were thought to re-animate some corpses. The mouth was filled with garlic so it could not bite anything.

Tiny seeds were scattered in the grave and churchyard as vampires were said to count every one. This would take so long that dawn would break and the vampire would have to return to the grave without having time to find a victim.

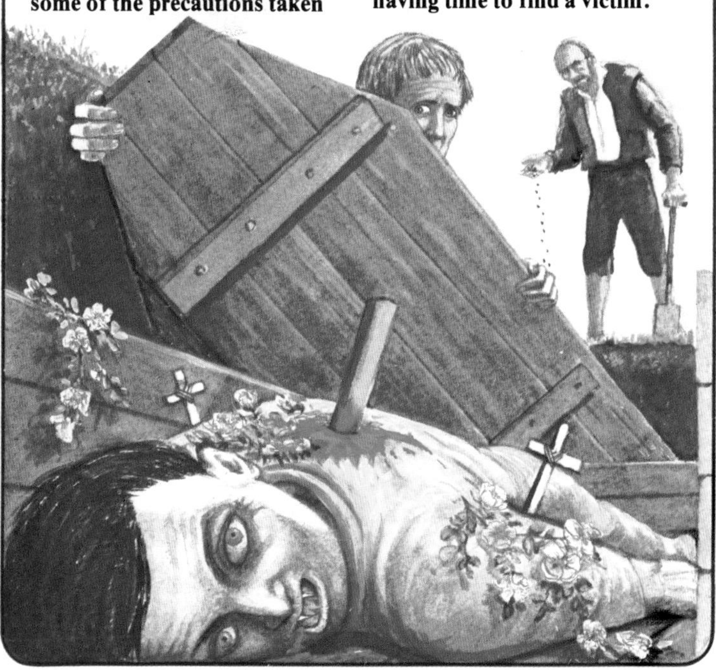

Plagues and vampires

Thousands of people were killed by the outbreaks of plague which swept Europe during the Middle Ages. It spread very quickly, with such terrible effects that normal life often ground to a halt. Buildings fell into disrepair, farming was neglected and people fled from infected areas if they could afford to. There was no cure for plague.

There were more reports of vampires during times of plague, and vampires were often blamed for spreading this terrible disease.

Plague was thought to hang in the air like a mist, so people tried to disturb it with loud noises, bells and music. The church bells that tolled for the dead were also believed to frighten away vampires.

Vampires were also scared off by large bonfires, known as need-fires. Animals were driven through the smoke and embers, and the ashes were scattered on the fields to protect them from the evil, plague-spreading vampires.

Plague victims had to be buried quickly because of the danger of infection. They were collected by the gravedigger and dumped into open pits outside the village. Infected houses had a cross marked on the door.

Disease was thought to be God's punishment for people's sins. The church offered protection from plague with special rituals and prayers. Processions went round villages sprinkling holy water and carrying crosses and pictures of the saints. These were thought to get rid of vampires and other demons.

Starving animals attacked and ate bodies flung in the burial pits. The blood-covered remains were blamed on vampires. One kind of plague caused a deep sleep that was easily mistaken for death, so some people were accidentally buried alive. These were the 'corpses' that did not rot and tried to escape the grave.

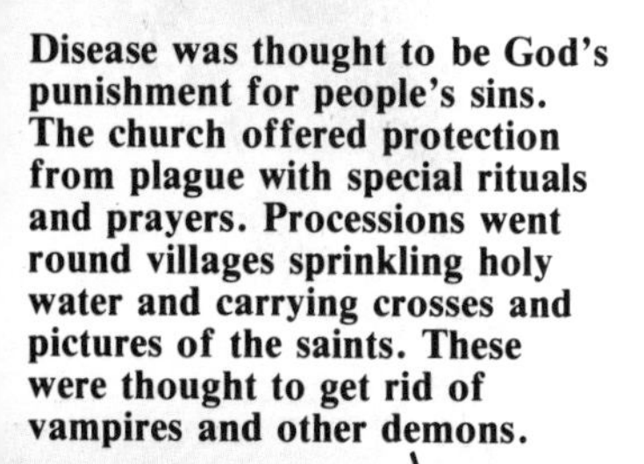

Herbs were burned to cover the stench of rotting bodies with sweet smells. The smoke was said to ward off vampires and destroy the plague in the air.

People believed the vampire spread plague and created new vampires with each attack, so the only way to end an epidemic of plague, or vampires, was by finding and destroying the vampire corpses. Many suspect bodies were staked, beheaded and burned to ashes in places hit by plague.

The story of Arnold Paole

In 1729 a young soldier from Serbia, named Arnold Paole, was sent to a remote and haunted part of Greece. One night he was viciously attacked by a vampire. He knew that unless he acted quickly he would die and become a vampire himself.

The only solution was for Arnold to find his attacker's grave, eat some earth from it and smear his body with the vampire's blood. Although he carried out this remedy, Arnold was so afraid that he left the army and returned to his home.

1. Arnold settled on his small farm in the village of Meduegna, and seemed to be quite unharmed. However, during the harvest he fell from a hay cart and died soon after. He was buried in the local churchyard, but did not rest there in peace.

2. Within a month Arnold was seen wandering the village at night. People who saw his spirit became very ill and four died within a few days. Panic spread and it was decided Arnold's body must be dug up and checked for any signs of vampirism.

3. This gruesome task was carried out one grey winter morning about ten weeks after Arnold's funeral. The gravedigger dug up the coffin, watched by officials from the capital city and army doctors as well as the local dignitaries.

4. When the coffin was opened, what it revealed made everyone certain they were dealing with a vampire. Arnold had moved to one side of the coffin. His hair and nails had grown and his mouth was red with fresh blood. He looked like a living man.

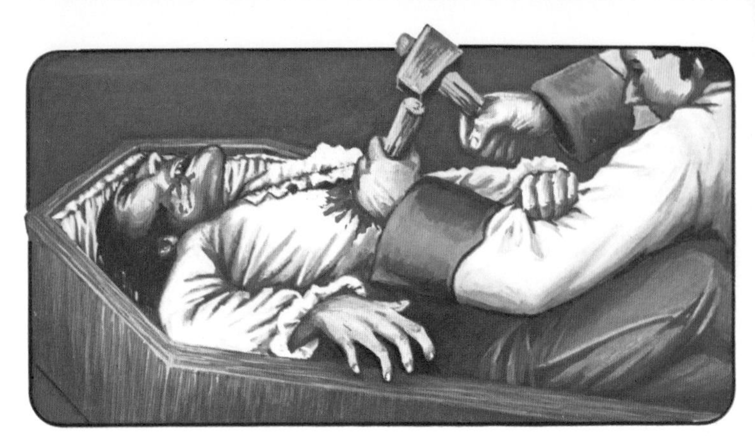

5. Arnold's corpse had to be dealt with in one of the traditional ways for ending vampirism before his soul could rest quietly. The villagers scattered garlic over Arnold's body and said prayers for his spirit. A stake of whitethorn wood was driven into his heart with one blow. Warm crimson blood gushed from the wound, as if Arnold were still alive—although he had been buried over two months. The corpse writhed in agony and let out a dreadful yell.

6. The four victims of Arnold's night time attacks were dug up in case they had become vampires too. The reports of this epidemic of the undead in Meduegna do not mention the condition of these corpses.

However, it seems they were vampires, as they were dealt with in the same way as Arnold had been: stabbed by whitethorn stakes and beheaded with a spade.

Finally all the vampires were thrown onto a roaring bonfire and burned in its fierce flames.

7. Fire was supposed to be the ultimate weapon for destroying vampires. A pile of smouldering ashes is impossibe to revive. Once deprived of an earthly home the vampire's soul was forced to go to the spirit world.

Although all the vampires had been staked, burned and reburied, within six years a new epidemic broke out in the village. Once again people were taken ill and became pale and weak as if from loss of blood.

They died suddenly just like Arnold's victims.

8. The villagers now knew how to deal with the danger, and another party of investigators arrived from Belgrade. They examined every suspicious grave and found many corpses in a vampiric state. These included children, and even small babies, as well as adults. All were full of fresh blood, so they were dealt with in the usual way. The ashes were thrown into a river to carry them away. People suspected the new epidemic had been caused by eating meat from animals once attacked by Arnold Paole.

Ghostly vampires

The most usual kind of vampire was a corpse brought back to life by a demon or by the original spirit, unable to rest in death. Sometimes the vampire was merely a spirit or ghost and did not need a body in its hunt for blood. This sort of vampire occurred most frequently where people worshipped and feared the spirits of dead ancestors.

Witches and sorcerers were thought to send out their souls to steal blood and do evil even before they died. Their bodies fell into a deep trance and did not recover until their souls returned.

▲The 'ekimmu' of Ancient Assyria were the ghosts of people who had not been properly buried. They became very hungry and thirsty and as no offerings had been made to them, they sucked the blood of the living. Their appearance meant certain death.

▲These hideous witches were the 'civateteo' from Mexico. Said to be the ghosts of women who died in childbirth, they stole babies to eat in revenge. They were thought to gather at crossroads so people left them offerings to save their children.

▲Australian aborigines saw blood as the strength of life and fed it to the sick. They also made blood-offerings to the spirits of dead relatives and cut themselves when in mourning. If the blood was not given freely the ghost grew angry and stole it.

An African elephant spirit

Many African tribes also made offerings of blood to the ghosts and spirits of their ancestors. Some spirits seemed to be happy with animal blood, but if they were not honoured by blood sacrifice they would return and spread illness and death among living relatives.

Ghosts became more unpleasant and dangerous the longer they were dead and it was important not to offend them. Sometimes the spirit returned as a ferocious man-eating animal.

The picture below shows the spirit with the trunk of an elephant said to haunt the Fan people of central Africa. Ghosts were sometimes said to cause death by eating the victim's heart or liver

Eastern vampires

There are many Chinese vampire legends, similar to those found in Europe. Some were said to be demons, but others were thought to be animated by the original souls, called the P'o. These were believed to remain on earth for a short time after death when they could turn their bodies into vampires.

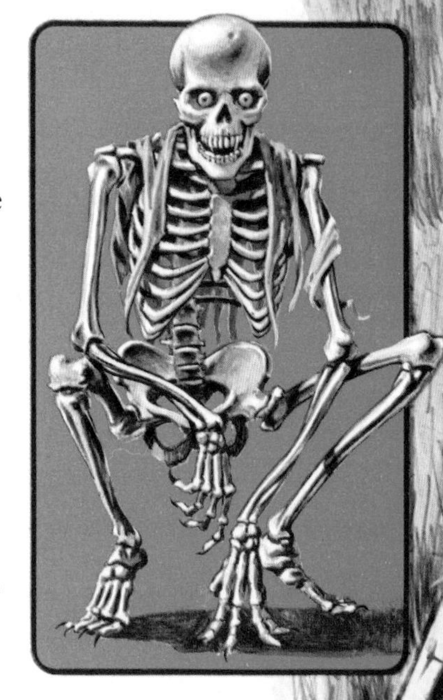

▶ Any corpse that did not rot was considered to have become a vampire. But even skeletons or just a skull could be possessed by demons and brought back to life. Chinese vampires often learned to fly and sometimes ate other corpses for food.

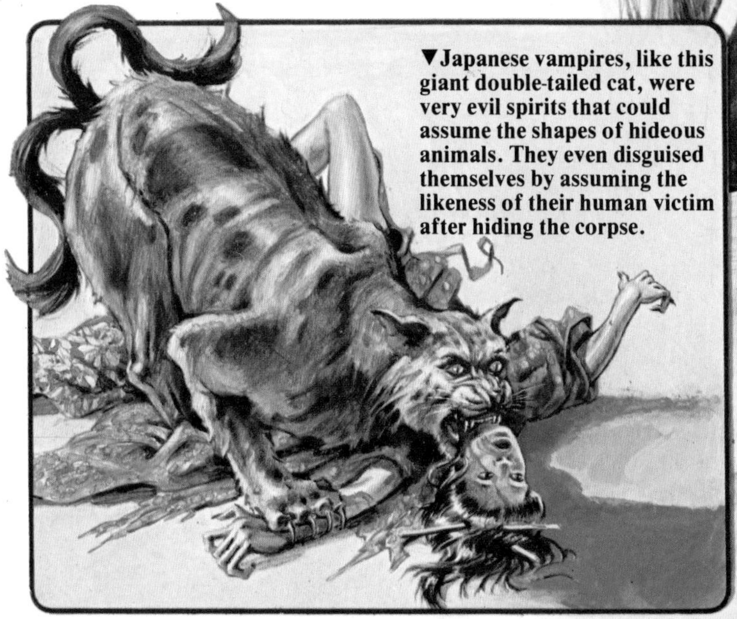

▼ Japanese vampires, like this giant double-tailed cat, were very evil spirits that could assume the shapes of hideous animals. They even disguised themselves by assuming the likeness of their human victim after hiding the corpse.

Liu, a vampire's victim

A teacher named Liu had just returned home after tending his ancestors' graves some distance away.

His wife went to wake him next morning, but, to her horror, found his corpse lying on the bed. It was completely drained of blood. A vampire had stolen the head to finish his feast of blood.

Liu's wife ran screaming from the house but was promptly arrested and put in jail.

On a nearby hillside a man gathering wood noticed a coffin lying neglected near an open grave.

People who came to investigate removed the lid of the coffin. Inside was the hideous vampire. It was covered in shaggy green hair and had sharp fangs and claws but a face like that of a living man. Liu's missing head was clutched tightly in the arms of the vampire.

Jungle vampires

There have been many stories of creatures returning from the dead in the jungles of Malaysia. Some of these vampire-like spirits were believed to be able to take the form of animals. Unlike European vampires, they were often created by magicians who used them to do evil.

According to legend, the Malaysian 'langsuir', shown here, was able to change into an owl. She was a woman who returned from the dead to attack children. She drank their blood through a hole in the back of her neck.

Demonic Vampires

▲ This tiny vampire, called the 'polong', was no bigger than the top joint of a man's little finger. It attacked people with the help of a demonic house cricket known as the 'pelesit'. This burrowed into the victim's body making an entrance for the polong to get in. They caused a terrible madness which often made the patient rave about cats.

The polong and pelesit were usually created by magic. The polong was made from the blood of a murdered man, kept in a bottle for a week while spells were said over it. The pelesit was made from the tongue of a dead baby. Oncc created these demons had to be fed on blood every day.

One of the most unpleasant demons of the Malasian jungles, shown below, was known as a 'bajang'. It was believed to take the form either of a polecat or a lizard.

Some bajangs were made out of the soul of a freshly buried child that had died at birth. A magician would visit the grave in the middle of the night and persuade the spirit to come out of the corpse by chanting magical spells.

Bajangs were suspected of attacking people when someone had a mysterious illness. The main symptoms of an attack by a bajang were fainting and convulsions. Like many vampirical beliefs, the supposed activities of a bajang served to explain any illness that people did not understand.

The way to destroy a bajang was to find its creator and destroy him. If the person suspected of controlling a bajang drowned in a river, the bajang, in the shape of a lizard, was said to escape through the nose of the drowning person.

Why believe in vampires?

Do vampires really exist? Up until the nineteenth century thousands of people all over the world thought that they did.

Now, we can explain the facts that started the vampire myth in more sensible ways.

Today, few people believe corpses can rise from their graves to attack the living and drink blood. This is not because we are more intelligent, but simply that life is so very different now.

In the past people were far more superstitious, but their belief in vampires was based on a great deal of evidence which seemed to have no other explanation.

Mysterious things seemed to happen in graveyards. Strange, dark figures were seen wandering among the tombstones at night, and frightening noises were heard coming from graves.

When people investigated, they sometimes found graves open and empty. Even more horrific were the coffins which contained twisted, blood-stained corpses, their shrouds all tattered and dirty. Others revealed life-like bodies which had remained quite unrotted in the grave. People thought they had discovered blood sucking vampires. It is more likely that these were the remains of people buried alive.

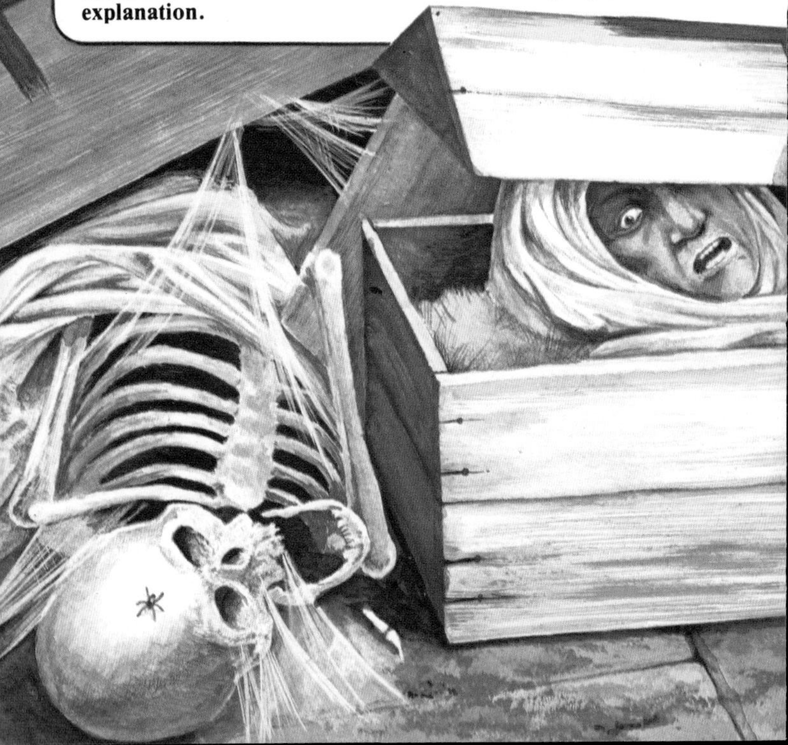

The picture on this page is based on a painting called 'Buried Alive', by the 19th century Belgian artist, Antoine Wiertz.

Premature burial has been common in the past and is not unknown even today. Sometimes it is quite difficult to be certain that a person is dead. One doctor suggested that the only way to be sure is to wait for the body to decompose.

A rare illness called catalepsy puts victims into a death-like trance of suspended animation, which can last for days or even weeks. The patient appears to be dead but if buried in this condition might wake in the coffin; only to die slowly of suffocation or starvation. Many must have tried to claw a way out of the grave and bitten at their own flesh in desperate hunger. No wonder these blood-filled coffins and horrific gory corpses started rumours of vampires.

The bodies that disappeared from graves had not climbed out in search of warm living blood to drink. They were more probably stolen by the 'Resurrection men'. These body snatchers stole fresh corpses and skeletons from their graves and sold them to doctors who wanted them for medical research.

The vampire in fiction

Stories about vampires have been written for thousands of years. Even Ancient Greek and Roman authors wrote about the dead who returned from the grave to drink blood.

The vampire theme proved so popular in eighteenth century Germany that many poets wrote ballads about ghostly vampires. These inspired later writers, such as Edgar Allan Poe and Bram Stoker, to produce horror stories that are still successful today.

Most recent vampire fiction has been written for films or for the theatre.

▲Lord Ruthven, an early stage vampire of the 1820s, was a character from a story 'The Vampyre'. This tale was begun by the English poet Lord Byron, but was completed by his friend Dr Polidori, who modelled the vampire on Byron.

Count Dracula

This classic tale of vampire horror was a success when it first appeared in 1897 and has not been out of print since. Dracula's author, Bram Stoker, had the idea for this story after a terrible nightmare. He researched the vampire legends of medieval Europe in the British Museum and decided to use Transylvania as a setting.

In the novel, the evil Count Dracula lives in a dark crumbling Transylvanian castle with a group of female vampires. However, he has bought an old abbey in England and plans to move there in order to spread vampirism throughout the land.

▲A young English lawyer, named Johnathan Harker, visits Dracula to arrange the transport for this move. Harker soon realizes that Dracula is a vampire. He is made a prisoner and the Count leaves for England.

Varney the Vampire

First published in 1847, this huge book was so popular that it was soon reprinted in 220 episodes, each selling for one penny. Its author, Thomas Prest, also wrote several other cheap 'penny dreadful' serials.

Varney the Vampire, subtitled 'The Feast of Blood', is set in England in the 1730s. It tells the tale of the Bannesworth family, plagued by a vampire named Sir Francis Varney.

Varney is basically a good person—but he was driven to evil by bad luck. He drinks the blood of Flora Bannesworth and kidnaps her lover. After many adventures Varney kills himself by jumping into the volcanic crater of Mount Vesuvius.

▼Dracula kills the entire crew of the ship to drink their blood and once in England he attacks Lucy Westenra. She dies and becomes a vampire, terrorizing London until a Dutch expert on vampires, Dr Van Helsing, drives a stake into her heart.

▲Harker escapes and helps Van Helsing search for Dracula, who has attacked Harker's wife. They chase the Count back to Transylvania, and plunge a knife deep into his vampire heart.

Introducing werewolves

Werewolves were evil, savage people with the power to turn themselves into wolves. Living on a diet of human flesh and blood, they roamed at night searching for lonely travellers to attack and eat.

Some were said to become creatures that were half man half wolf, others to change into wolves completely. It was believed that a werewolf could turn his skin inside out to hide the fur when in human form. Many people accused of being werewolves had their bodies ripped open in the hunt for this wolf fur.

It was, however, possible to recognize the werewolf in his human shape. Werewolves were supposed to be very hairy, with straight bushy eyebrows that met in the middle and small pointed ears. Often the third finger of each hand was as long as the second, and hair grew in the palms of the hands.

Traditionally the werewolf returned to human shape once it had been injured and could be traced by the trail of blood it left behind. The most effective way to kill a werewolf was with a bullet or knife made from the silver of a melted crucifix. The corpse had to be burned rather than buried, as it was believed a werewolf would rise from its grave as a vampire.

Legends tell of men turned into werewolves by a curse or dreadful accident. Doomed to become wolves each night or with every full moon, they welcomed death as a release from this fate.

People all over the world have believed in werewolves, and a rare mental illness called lycanthropy was also recognized in ancient times. This disease makes patients think that they can turn into wolves, although they do not. However, they usually behave like werewolves, murdering people and eating the flesh of their victims.

Becoming a werewolf

Some people were believed to turn into wolves during a full moon against their will. However, some bad people actually wanted to become ferocious werewolves and they used magic to bring about the transformation.

A Russian legend said it was necessary to jump over a fallen tree in the forest, stab it with a small copper knife and chant a spell to become a wolf. Drinking water that collected in a wolf's paw print or eating the brains of an animal killed by wolves were sure ways of changing into a wolf.

In many parts of Europe, legends grew up about exactly what sort of magic acts were supposed to be able to turn somebody into a wolf.

A typical magical werewolf ritual is shown below.

▲A would-be-werewolf made his transforming ointment at midnight when the moon was full. He put wolfsbane, opium, foxgloves, bat blood and fat of a murdered child into a pot and boiled them.

▲When this nasty mixture was ready the werewolf took off his clothes and rubbed the ointment into his skin. He put on his pelt of wolf fur, chanting spells and incantations, asking the wolf spirit to turn him into a wolf.

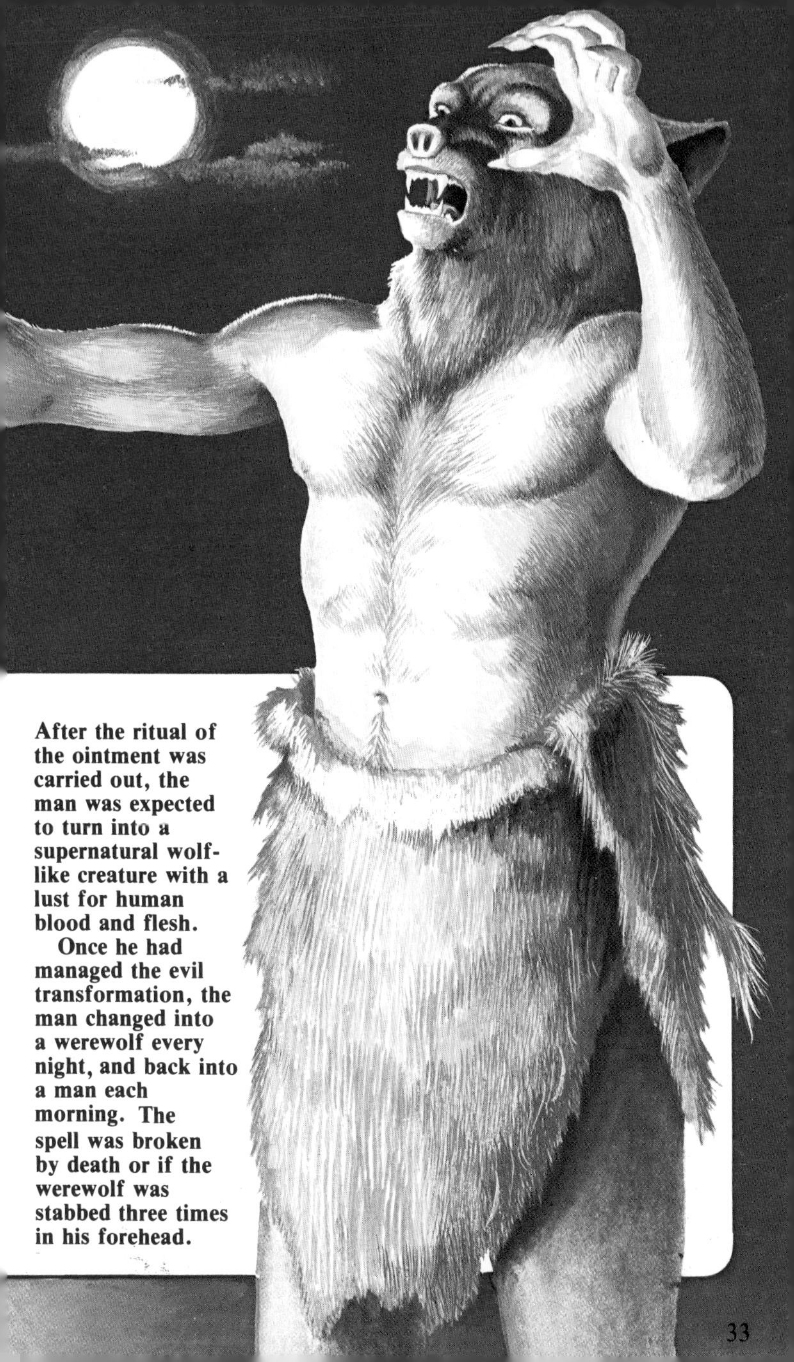

After the ritual of the ointment was carried out, the man was expected to turn into a supernatural wolf-like creature with a lust for human blood and flesh.

Once he had managed the evil transformation, the man changed into a werewolf every night, and back into a man each morning. The spell was broken by death or if the werewolf was stabbed three times in his forehead.

European werewolves

Stories of werewolves sprang up in most countries where real wolves were a danger to the population. There have been very few wolves in Britain since the Middle Ages, and the last wild wolf was hunted down some time in the 18th century.

The discovery of a real, but rare, strange disease called 'lycanthropy' increased the terror of the legend of the werewolf. Anyone suffering from lycanthropy believed himself to be a werewolf.

This form of insanity sometimes lead to people trying to act as if they were real wolves. In France especially, there were many trials of people accused of lycanthropy.

▼These fearsome Norse warriors, known as the Berserkers, added a great deal to the werewolf legends of Europe. They wore wild animal skins and grew long hair and beards to give themselves a frightening appearance.

Isolated villagers attacked by these murderous invaders probably thought they were half animal. The Berserkers were said to be able to turn into ferocious bears and wolves during battles.

◀A Norse saga tells how a wizard put a spell on two wolf skins, so whoever wore them became wolves for ten days. These skins were discovered by two warriors, Sigmund and Sinjoth, who took shelter in a forest cabin. Unaware of the curse, they stole the hides from the men asleep there.

Once put on, the skins would not come off. Sigmund and Sinjoth howled and attacked the sleeping men and even bit each other. They broke the spell by burning the skins when they fell off ten days later.

▶According to an Irish story, a priest who was lost in some woods found a wolf sitting by a fire. It spoke in a human voice and asked the priest to give the last sacraments to his wife, who was dying. The wolf explained that his family had been cursed, so one man and one woman had to spend seven years as wolves. If they were alive after this time they could become human again.

The priest did not believe the story until the she-wolf ripped open her wolf skin to reveal her true shape as a woman.

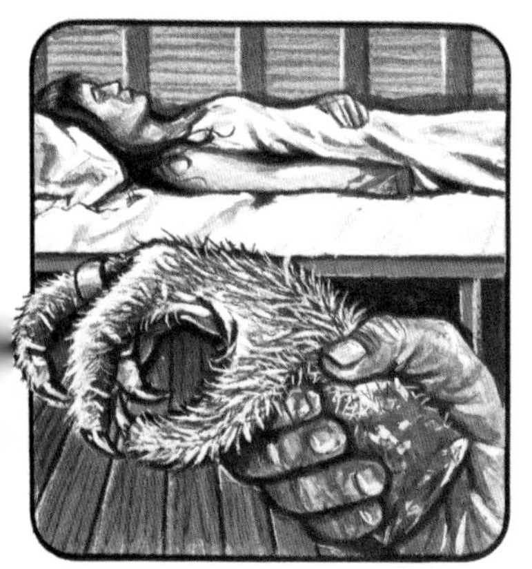

◀France has many legends about werewolves. One medieval story tells of a hunter who fought off a huge wolf that attacked him in the forest. He slashed off one of its forepaws, but the beast escaped and the hunter put the paw in his bag. Returning home, he was amazed to find it was changing into a woman's hand.

He recognized a ring on one finger as one he had given to his wife. Rushing upstairs, he found her lying in bed, bleeding from many sword cuts with a stump where her hand was missing.

A French wolf-boy

In 1604 Jean Grenier, a 13 year-old French boy, was accused of being a werewolf. He claimed a mysterious man, the Lord of the Forest, had given him a magic wolf skin and ointment that turned him into a wolf. For three years he ran about the forest as a man-eating werewolf.

1. Jean Grenier admitted eating more than 50 children. He had a craving for raw human flesh and found little girls most delicious. When very hungry he would even attack a crowd of people.

Passing through a village one day he found a baby sleeping in an empty house. Jean could not resist such a tasty meal and as no-one was in sight dragged the child from its cradle.

He carried it off to the woods and shared the bloody remains with a real wolf that joined him later.

2. Another child had more luck. He was playing at the edge of the wood when Jean attacked suddenly. The werewolf leaped out of a dense thicket and, hurling himself at the boy knocked him to the ground and snapped at his throat. The boy would have been torn apart if his cries had not been heard by his uncle, who was nearby.

The boy's uncle rushed up shouting at Jean 'I'll get you now'. Eventually he managed to beat off the werewolf with his heavy stick.

3. One afternoon three girls out tending their sheep found Jean lurking in some sand dunes. His strange appearance frightened them very much. He was thin and dirty, dressed only in rags. His thick hair was matted, his teeth and nails like those of an animal rather than a boy and his eyes were wild and ferocious. The oldest girl asked why his skin was so dark. Jean replied it was because he was a werewolf and if the sun were to set he would eat them. The three girls immediately ran away in terror.

4. Jean Grenier was proud of his adventures as a werewolf and bragged about them to a girl named Marguerite Poirier. She told her parents that Jean scared her but they thought little of her stories until she was attacked herself. Marguerite said that a wild beast, like a wolf but with red fur and a stumpy tail, had leaped upon her. It ripped her clothes with its fangs, but she beat if off with her staff. The beast was so frightening that Marguerite ran home as fast as possible.

5. The attack on Marguerite led to Jean Grenier's arrest and trial before the parliament of Bordeaux. Jean claimed that he was a werewolf and confessed that he had murdered and eaten people. His accounts of the attacks were the same as those of the witnesses and victims. Marguerite was the only one who thought he had been in the form of a wolf but there was no doubt that he was a murderous cannibal. Two doctors were called in and said Jean was suffering from lycanthropy.

6. The judge thought Jean was so dull and idiotic that any child half his age had more sense. He discounted rumours of witchcraft and shape-changing and sentenced Jean to spend the rest of his life in a monastery at Bordeaux.

After being taken there Jean still behaved like an animal, running on all fours and eating any raw meat he could find. The judge visited Jean seven years later and found him less wild–but still claiming to have been a werewolf.

Werewolves in America

North America has many legends of people who could turn into animals, but not all of them were werewolves.

The ancient Indian stories often tell of marriages between people and animals. Usually the animal could remove its skin and was a man or woman underneath.

Some tribes believed they were descended from such a marriage and so were related to a particular animal. Some warriors were even said to send their spirits out in the body of an animal and would die if it was harmed.

▲Canadian Indians who pretended to believe in Christianity were said to become werewolves. According to legend, they turned their skins inside out at night to change into wolves and then went off into the woods to attack true Christians.

◄Canada was colonized by many French people, who brought with them their belief in the werewolf. Giant supernatural wolves were thought to dig up graves at night to eat the people buried there. The werewolf was believed to be transformed by God as a punishment for not going to mass for seven years. He would roam the forest each night until blessed by a priest or killed by a silver bullet.

Newspaper reports in July and December, 1767, told of a werewolf that was seen in the area of Saint Roche, Quebec. During the day he was supposed to be a beggar and at night he was said to change into a giant bloodthirsty wolf.

The Nootka wolf cults

▲Each winter, during a full moon, the Indians of the north-west coast of America initiate young warriors into secret wolf cults. The Nootka tribe call this ceremony the 'Kulwana' and members of the society act the part of wolves. They wear a blanket tied at the forehead to form a snout because the wolf mask like the one above may only be worn by a chief. Young Nootkas are tested for endurance and bravery.

The Nootkas have a myth about the origins of the 'Kulwana'. They say that four brothers fled to Nootka Island when their tribe was wiped out in a war with neighbours. The youngest, Ha-Sass, sought knowledge from the wolves, who were said to know everything. He disguised himself in a seal skin, draining his blood so the wolves would not smell his human scent. The wolves found him and took him to their lair to eat.

When Ha-Sass revealed himself they admired his cunning so much that they taught him the wolf dances and rituals so he would become strong like them. The wolves wore masks of men (pictured left) for these magic ceremonies. After four days of training they gave Ha-Sass an enchanted club and sent him home to teach his brothers and other young men the secrets of the wolf power.

The Navaho wolf-men

The Navaho Indians of the south-western USA had a strong belief in magic and witchcraft and a great fear of the dead. Witches often dug up corpses to steal the treasures buried with them and take parts of dead bodies to make into magic poisons.

Witches were called 'human wolves' as they disguised themselves with mountain lion and wolf-skins. Some were even thought to turn into animals. The story here is an old Navaho legend about the terrible human wolves.

1. A Navaho girl and her small brother were travelling to fetch corn for their family. The girl knew they were being followed by human wolves so she sent her brother home on the horse. She hid in a thicket but was discovered by the human wolves.

2. The girl's oldest brother was hunting nearby and heard the wolves howling and his sister screaming. By the time he reached the thicket she had been carried away by the human wolves. He found bloody tracks and decided to follow them.

3. These tracks led to an opening in the face of a cliff. The boy entered and found a long dark passage cut from the stone. It went deep into the cliff and led to a cave full of human wolves. The boy hid in a small room littered with bones and treasure.

4. The human wolves soon found the boy and took him to their chief, who was large and fat, singing a song. He said the boy must either be put to death or become a human wolf. The boy decided to join them and try to escape later. They gave him some meat to eat. He knew it was human flesh, but did not know it came from his sister's body. She had been eaten by the human wolves, who had thrown her bones into a corner. He hid the meat, planning to feed it to the guard dogs later.

5. The boy waited for everyone to fall asleep, then crept past the dogs. The passage had been blocked but he managed to get outside and hide in a badger hole. The human wolves chased the boy but he was so well hidden they did not see him.

6. Two days later the boy reached home and learned of his sister's murder by the human wolves. On his way to the next war dance, he saw the human wolf chief riding a horse. The boy shot an arrow into his back and the wolf chief was killed.

Relatives of the werewolf

There are stories of people changing into almost every known animal, from sheep and birds to insects and fish. Any animal that was once a human is called a werebeast.

The transformations were not always evil, as with the werewolf,

Some took place after death, when the spirit returned to Earth as an animal. Some people even believed that animals could turn themselves into human beings if they wanted to.

The werefoxes of China and Japan were animals that became humans to trick and harm ordinary people. To do this a fox had to be 500 years old and live in a graveyard.

Ancient Scandinavian sagas say that Odin, the god of war, gave the Berserkers their wild strength and bravery in battle. However, he punished any cowardly warriors by turning them into wild boars.

A German bishop named Hatto was said to have been gnawed to death by a swarm of wererats. They were the souls of hundreds of starving peasants that he had murdered.

Welsh witches were supposed to change into hares and drink all the milk from cows, leaving them dry when the farmer tried to milk them. They were also accused of casting evil spells that turned innocent people into animals, and of becoming man-eating werewolves when they died.

A sad Norwegian legend tells how Prince Bjorn terrorized the country as a huge bear, after being transformed by his wicked stepmother. He ate so many sheep that his father sent hunters to kill him, not realizing the bear was his own son. The stepmother cooked the body and served it at a celebration banquet.

Wild werebeasts

Werewolf stories were most common in Europe and North America, places where real wolves were often the most terrifying animals. In other parts of the world there have been tales of people turning into lions, tigers, crocodiles, and even into snakes.

In Africa the souls of village chiefs and other important people were thought to take the form of noble animals. When someone was attacked by a lion,

they would often try to reason with it—believing the animal contained the old chief's soul. Wicked people were sometimes said to be transformed into unpleasant animals. The scavenging hyena, for example, was thought to be a fitting end for certain African witches.

According to one old Indian legend, people who did not pay their debts turned into monkeys and ran off to hide in the trees.

Introducing demons

European vampires and werewolves, though supernatural and evil, were at least partly human. People became vampires or werewolves, so it was said, as a result of their wicked actions. The kind of spirit that encouraged evil was often more bizarre than the vampires or werewolves themselves.

For many years spirits called demons or devils were blamed for many of the misfortunes of life. Demons were not ghosts, as they had never been living human beings. Some people thought they were angels that had been expelled from heaven for rebelling against God. Others simply said they were elemental spirits—a form of supernatural life that took pleasure in destroying all that was good in the world.

The illustration above shows a medieval demon playing on a trumpet to attract the attention of possible converts to his evil ways. Angels were supposed to protect people from demons, and they too played music, but not always successfully.

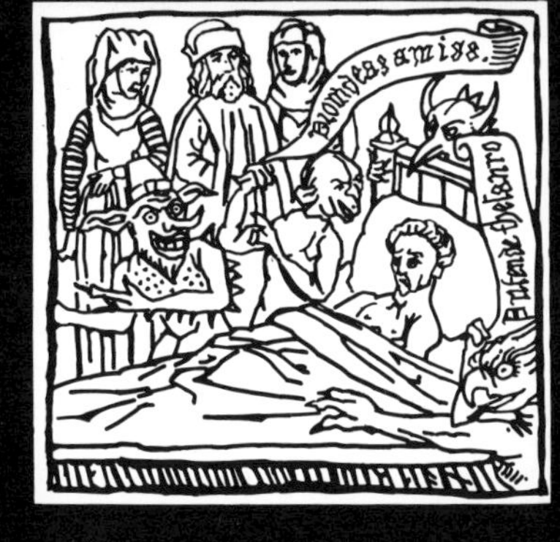

Though demons were interested in influencing the world of the living, they were even more keen on gaining control of a person's soul after death. The rather gruesome illustration at the top of the page shows some demons waiting at the bedside of a dying person. They were supposed to drag the soul down to hell as the last breath was drawn.

Though many demons lived in hell, where they were said to thrive in a world of flames and tortured souls, they were seen by ordinary mortals during the hours of darkness. Sometimes demons offered a lifetime free from money worries in return for a person's soul. People who sold their souls to the devil signed a contract using their own blood as ink. Once this was done they could not escape unless a priest was able to release them from the devil's power with a prayer.

Some of the more mischievous demons were said to jump into the open mouths of people when they yawned. The only way to get the demon out of someone was to ask a priest to sprinkle holy water on the poor sufferer.

Medieval demons

Here are some of the many demons that were believed to haunt Europe throughout the Middle Ages. They ranged from evil old women, said to be witches, to dragons.

This Scandinavian dragon was called 'Niohoggr', which means 'Corpse tearer'. He was believed to carry off the dead with his sharp claws, devouring them in his lair deep beneath the earth.

Red Caps were bloodthirsty Scottish elves. They kept their caps red by dipping them in blood, obtained by throwing big boulders at passers-by.

During the plague-ridden Middle Ages, Death was pictured as a grinning human skeleton. He came suddenly to take people from the things they loved most.

People also believed the air was inhabited by over seven million demons. They haunted at night, could easily be swallowed, and animated corpses as vampires.

Demons formed an army of evil under the leadership of the devil. Each regiment had a captain; this one is Eurynome, the prince of death, who fed on human corpses.

Witches were thought to have magic powers from the devil. They spread disease, conjured up storms, changed into animal shapes and became vampires.

Demon ghosts and gods

Some demons were gods, like Kali and Xipe Totec, shown here, who could be very evil.

It is because demons were supposed to be beyond the laws of nature that they could create their bodies out of thin air or disguise themselves either as humans or animals.

▲This is Xipe Totec, a Mexican demon with a taste for blood. He was said to suck it from sinners who fell asleep in hell and the prisoners of war bled to death in sacrifice to him. Xipe Totec was believed to appear on earth wherever blood was spilt.

◀Kali is the Hindu Goddess of destruction, plague and violent death. Here she is holding the head of Raktivira, the king of the demons. He and Kali fought a savage battle, but Kali managed to kill Raktivira by stabbing him and drinking all his blood.

▶In the Caribbean Islands some vultures, known as Loogaroos, were said to be the ghosts of evil witches who had made pacts with the devil. He gave the witches magic powers while they were alive but when they died forced them to provide him with a daily supply of fresh blood.

At night the vultures removed their skins and flew off as spirits in search of victims. If the Loogaroo skin was found it was ground up with pepper and salt so the witch could not put it on and would be destroyed.

►This strange creature is one of the Rakshasas. They were evil Indian demons that haunted burial grounds, animated dead bodies and terrorized priests. Rakshasas had great supernatural powers and could transform themselves into any shape they liked. Often they took on ugly deformed bodies with a crazy mixture of limbs in odd colours like blue, yellow, red or green.

These bloodthirsty demons were extremely dangerous. Their long nails were poisonous and they loved to eat human flesh, and sometimes even each other.

◄This Japanese demon also liked to eat people. It is one of the Kappas that lived in rivers and lakes and pulled into the water anyone silly enough to get close to them. There were only two ways of escaping a Kappa's jaws. The first was to feed it cucumber or melon, which Kappas loved so much they did not bother with tasteless humans. The other was by bowing to it. The Kappas were so polite they always bowed back, spilling the liquid stored in the top of their heads, which gave them their supernatural powers.

►The Yara-Ma were demons which haunted the forests of Australia. They were small creatures, with scaly red and green skin and suckers instead of hands and feet. They hid in the branches of trees waiting for someone to sit in the shade beneath. Then the Yara-Ma leaped down, fixed its suckers to the victim, and drank his blood.

They had such huge mouths they could swallow a human being in one gulp. Occasionally, if the Yara-Ma went to sleep after his meal, his dinner might manage to climb out and run away.

'Vampires' from history

History is full of bloodthirsty tyrants, though perhaps none so frightening as Prince Vlad Dracula, or the Countess Elizabeth of Bathory.

Their histories read like the vampire legends of central Europe come to life.

Vlad the impaler

For part of the 15th century Prince Vlad Dracula ruled a small country called Wallachia. It is now part of the region of Transylvania in Romania. Bram Stoker probably based his fictional vampire count on Vlad Dracula, who was feared throughout Europe for his bloodthirsty deeds.

We know a great deal about Vlad Dracula's life and adventures as they were widely reported at the time and many of these records still survive.

He was usually known as 'Vlad the Impaler', a nickname he earned by impaling thousands of people on wooden stakes. This is a particularly nasty form of execution as the stakes were oiled and rounded at the ends. This way they did not cause gaping wounds and so death was slow and very painful.

He was also accused of skinning, roasting, boiling and chopping up people as if they were ingredients for a stew, and even of feeding the remains to the victims' families. It is said that he nailed hats to the heads of nobles who refused to remove them in respect for his rank.

In spite of his evil behaviour Dracula was sometimes described in Wallachia as a 'cruel but just ruler'. He was even seen as a hero because he drove out the Turkish armies that invaded Europe during the 15th century.

After one battle against Turkish invaders, Prince Dracula impaled an entire detachment of prisoners. On another occasion, he had 300 prisoners burned alive. In 1476, at the age of 46, Vlad was beheaded and buried in a monastery.

Elizabeth of Bathory

In 1611 the Hungarian countess Elizabeth of Bathory was bricked into one room of her castle as a punishment for killing over 650 young girls. She had murdered them for their blood which she bathed in, believing it would restore her youth and beauty.

The countess was very vain and feared growing old and losing the beauty for which she was famed throughout Europe. She discovered the magic blood cure when she hit a maid so hard that blood gushed from her nose all over Elizabeth's face and hands. She was convinced the blood had made her skin more lovely and decided to bath her whole body in it. The unfortunate maid was killed and her blood drained into a tub and gently warmed. This was the start of ten years of cruel murders for the hundreds of girls lured to the castle by promises of money and jobs. Instead, they were locked up and tortured, kept alive for as long as possible to be milked of their blood at dawn for the countess's beauty baths.

▼ Bran castle is close to the scene of one of Vlad Dracula's most bloodthirsty massacres. It is visited today by tourists searching for the truth about the Dracula legend.

Supernatural cinema

People love to be scared, which is why horror films are so very popular. They give a realistic setting to things we know are impossible.

On film we see the vampire in all his gory glory, fangs bared ready to sink into the throat of his next victim. Before our very eyes, a man turns into a furry wolf and lopes into the misty forest in search of human flesh. In the end good always triumphs over evil. The vampire is destroyed by a stake through the heart and the werewolf must be shot with a silver bullet.

▼ Bela Lugosi, the first famous screen Dracula, was actually born in Romania, traditional home of the vampire.

He began playing the Vampire Count in 1927 on the stage. A nurse was at every performance in case any of the audience were overcome by fright.

When he died in 1956, Bela Lugosi was buried wrapped in the black cloak, lined with red satin, that he had worn so often as Dracula.

The Prince of Darkness

An English company, Hammer Films, became the leading makers of horror films in the mid 1950s. They re-made many old horror classics in colour, using spectacular special effects and a great deal more blood than had been seen before.

Christopher Lee succeeded Bela Lugosi as the classic undead count after Hammer's first vampire film 'Dracula' was released in 1958.

On the right Christopher Lee is shown baring his fangs at his victims in the 1965 Hammer Films production 'Dracula, Prince of Darkness'. In this film the count is finally destroyed by being thrown into the ice-covered moat of his castle.

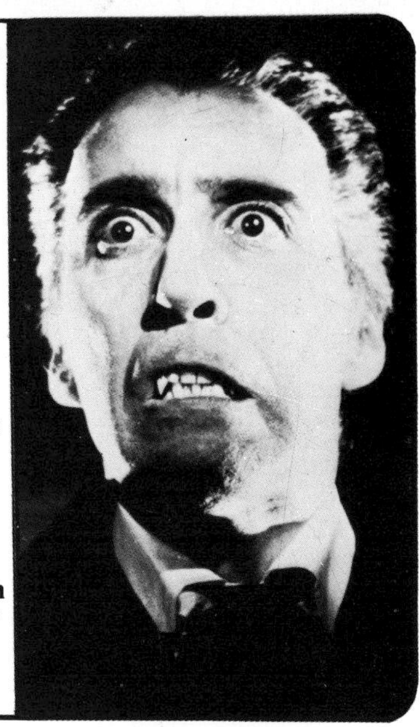

'Nosferatu'

This is the Vampire Count dissolving in a shaft of dawn sunlight in the first film version of Bram Stoker's novel 'Dracula'. The title of the film, made in 1922, was 'Nosferatu'—a Romanian word meaning the undead.

Movie horrors

Horror films have been made about many strange creatures besides vampires, including machine-like monsters and all kinds of werebeasts.

The picture below shows a zombie leaving his grave in the 1966 Hammer film 'Plague of the Zombies'. A zombie is a corpse brought to life by magic to act as a slave for its master.

In this film, set in south-west England, a local landowner puts an army of zombies to work in his tin mines. Instead of providing free labour, the zombies are blown to bits in an explosion when the squire's plans are foiled by the hero.

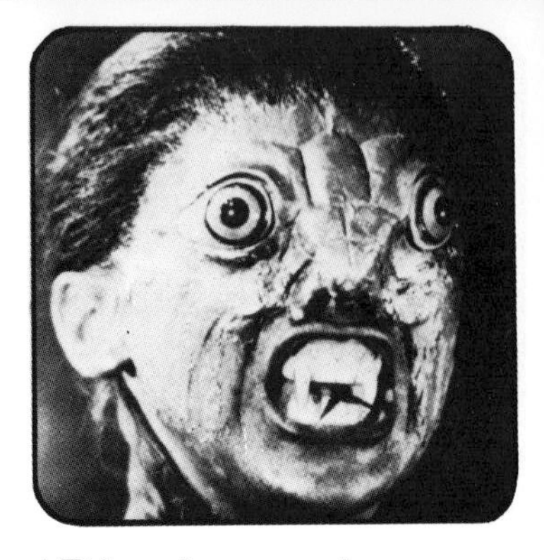

▲This snake woman from Hammer's film 'The Reptile' is a normal girl turned into a huge snake by a curse. She eats living animals but prefers to feed on people and even kills her father before being burnt to death.

▲'The Legend of the Werewolf', made by Tyburn Films, is about a baby reared by wolves. He grows up as a wolf-man and transforms at each full moon. He commits many foul murders, until he is hunted down and shot.

Monster make-up

The stars of horror films have to wear strange make-up in order to appear gruesome.

Vampires are dusted with a green powder to produce a corpse-like complexion. Their fake fangs are specially made by dentists. Christopher Lee wore red-coloured contact lenses to make his eyes look wild and blood-filled.

The werewolf's make-up is even more difficult. When Lon Chaney Jr played 'The Wolf Man' in 1941, hundreds of yak hairs were glued to his face to create a wolfish effect. It took a whole day and 21 changes of make-up to film the sequence showing him change into a wolf-man.

Supernatural guide

Throughout this book you will have met most of the important characters in the supernatural world of vampires, werewolves and demons. On these pages we list some of the other nasty creatures of this strange world, as well as some of the plants and animals connected with these dreadful legends.

BAT: Vampire bats live in dark places such as caves or hollow trees in many parts of central and south America. They were named after the bloodsucking vampires of legend as they are nocturnal creatures and live on the blood of other animals.

Vampire bats rarely attack humans but as their bites are fairly painless they can often drink the blood of a sleeping animal without it realizing.

BRUXAS: A female vampire from Portugal who flew out at night in the form of a bird. She drank the blood of her own children and terrified lonely travellers.

DHAMPIR: According to ancient Transylvanian legends the son of a vampire, known as a dhampir, was the only person who could see or kill the invisible vampires.

DRACUL: This is the Romanian word for devil or dragon. Vlad the Impaler was called Dracula because his father's name was Dracul and putting an 'a' on the end of a Romanian word makes it mean 'son of'. 'Dracula', therefore, actually means 'Son of the Devil'.

FAMILIAR: The pet of a witch, kept specially to help her in magical rituals. The most usual kind of animal familiar was a cat. There are stories of witches using toads, blackbirds and almost every other kind of small animal, and even, sometimes, demons.

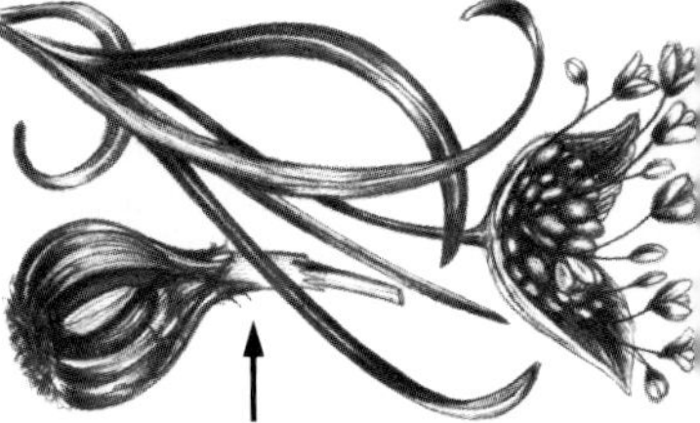

GARLIC: A relative of the onion plant that is often used for seasoning food. It has also been used in many different ways as a protection against evil spirits, including vampires. An ancient Islamic legend says that garlic sprang up on the spot where Satan first put his foot after being expelled from paradise.

HARPIES: These female monsters were winged hags said to haunt the ancient Greeks. They carried living people away to hell and devoured shipwrecked sailors.

ITZPAPALOTL: A frightening Aztec demon who was a cross between a woman and a butterfly. Stone knives surrounded her wings and her tongue itself was a knife. She also had a magic cloak which she used to change herself into a harmless-looking butterfly.

JARACACA: An evil Brazilian vampire in the form of a snake. It was said to steal a mother's milk while she was feeding her child. At the same time the Jaracaca would put its tail in the mouth of the child.

JIGAR-KHOR: This was one of the many blood-drinking witches and spirits that were said to haunt the jungles of India. Jigar-khors were female spirits that were supposed to be able to steal their victims' livers simply by staring at them while reciting a magic spell.

KELPIE: A Scottish demon in the shape of a horse. Anyone who found a Kelpie lurking by the bank of a river and tried to ride it across the water found it impossible to get off again. The Kelpie always drowned its victims before eating them.

LAMIA: A vampire-like demon with the face of a beautiful woman but the body of a snake. According to Greek legends, Lamia fattened up young men before she devoured them.

MANDRAKE: This small plant was thought to have evil powers, as it was said to grow beneath the gallows where it could be nourished by the flesh and blood of the criminal hanging above. It was dangerous to pick, as the plant let out a scream when pulled from the ground that killed anyone who heard it.

MARA: A Danish vampire that was a beautiful woman during the day—but who sucked the blood from young men at night. Anyone who fell in love with her would suffer terrible feelings of suffocation and strangling, but she could be frightened away by a knife.

NEED-FIRES: Fires that were supposed to be able to drive away evil spirits. They were lit during catastrophies of many kinds throughout the Middle Ages and especially at times of plague. Need-fires had to be started at night, either by rubbing two pieces of wood together or else with a lighted twig from another need-fire.

OWENGAS: Vampires from Guinea in Northern Africa that were the bad spirits of evil ancestors or of dead magicians in a physical form. Belief in owengas led to the practice of clearing up all spilt blood and destroying any blood-stained objects in order to deprive them of their food.

SATAN: According to the Jewish and Christian traditions, Satan was a senior angel who lead a revolt against God. For his punishment, he was sent to hell, from where he directs a battle against all that is good in the world.

STRIGES: These Greek demons flew about at night as birds and snatched sleeping children from their cradles to eat their flesh and drink their blood.

THAYE TASE: One type of Burmese demon known generally as tases. They appear especially when there is an epidemic of cholera or smallpox and haunt those who are about to die, by giggling and laughing at their victim's pain. Like vampires, they are said to be the souls of people who have died a violent death.

VAMPIRE: The word probably comes from an old Turkish word 'oupir', meaning 'bloodsucker'.

Apart from ordinary vampires, such as Arnold Paole and the fictional Count Dracula, we have shown 19 different types of vampire in this book. There are so many strange legends throughout the world, and the imaginations of superstitious people are so powerful, that there have probably been many more kinds of vampire than we have included here.

VRYKOLAKAS: In Greek vampire legends, this ugly creature is the corpse of an evil man brought to life by a devil. The vrykolakas sat on its sleeping victims and killed them by suffocation.

WILLS-O'-THE-WISP: Glowing lights that can sometimes be seen at night hovering above rotting vegetation. When plants decay they can give off a gas that burns of its own accord. Before they were properly understood, these lights were the subject of many strange superstitions.

According to one old Chinese legend, Wills-o'-the-wisp were vampire-like evil spirits that grew out of spilt blood, or out of the rotting wood of coffins. They were said to make people ill and to ruin crops by burning the ears of corn. Like vampires, they only came out at night.

WOLF: Once common throughout Europe and North America, this animal that has inspired so many strange legends is now limited to remote areas.

The last wild wolves in Britain were killed in the eighteenth century. Although they kill other animals, it is very rare for wolves to attack humans.

ZOTZ: A South American demon in the legends of the Mayan people. The Zotz was an ugly winged creature with the head of a dog. It lived in a part of hell and drank the blood of anyone who passed through its territory.

Index